Baby J Says NO!

A book that teaches kids how to recognize and say "No!" to sexual abuse.

Written by Jack Nunnery

Illustrations by Kate Collazo

Baby J Says NO!

A book that teaches children how to recognize and say "NO!" to sexual abuse.

For the kids of the world.
May they always know they have the
power and courage to speak up
against sexual abuse.

Hi, I'm Baby J!

Today, I'm going to share what you should do if someone wants to touch your private parts.

What are your private parts?

Your private parts are the parts on your body that get covered by your bathing suit.

Boys and Girls have different kinds of private parts

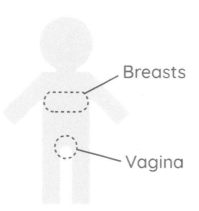

A girl's privates are called the breast, the vagina and the bottom.

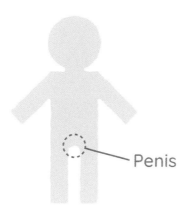

A boy's private parts are called the penis and the bottom.

Private parts are special parts of your body. And when it comes to your body, there are rules.

The rules are simple and will help keep you safe.

They are called,

"TOUCHING RULES."

There are two Touching Rules.

Here are the two Touching Rules...

TOUCHING RULE

No one should ever touch your private parts.

TOUCHING RULE

No one should ever ask you to touch their private parts.

If someone breaks the Touching Rules, it is your job to shout,

"No!"

Let's practice shouting, "No!"

On the count of three, shout it out loud and strong. One...two...three...

Good job! Let's keep practicing. If someone touches your private parts, what can you say?

If someone promises to give you candy or ice cream to touch your private parts, what can you say?

Right!
Let's keep going.

Now, when someone asks you to
take your clothes off to
look at your private parts,
what can you say?

You're doing great!

What if someone asks you to look at their private parts, what can you say?

No!

And if someone asks you to touch their private parts, what can you say?

Right!

Now, if someone wants to take pictures of you with no clothes on, what can you say?

If someone wants to show you pictures of naked people on the computer, what can you say?

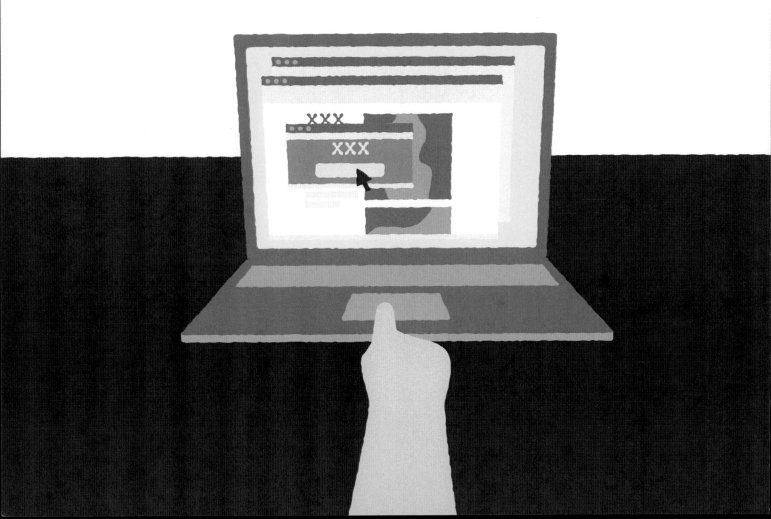

NO!

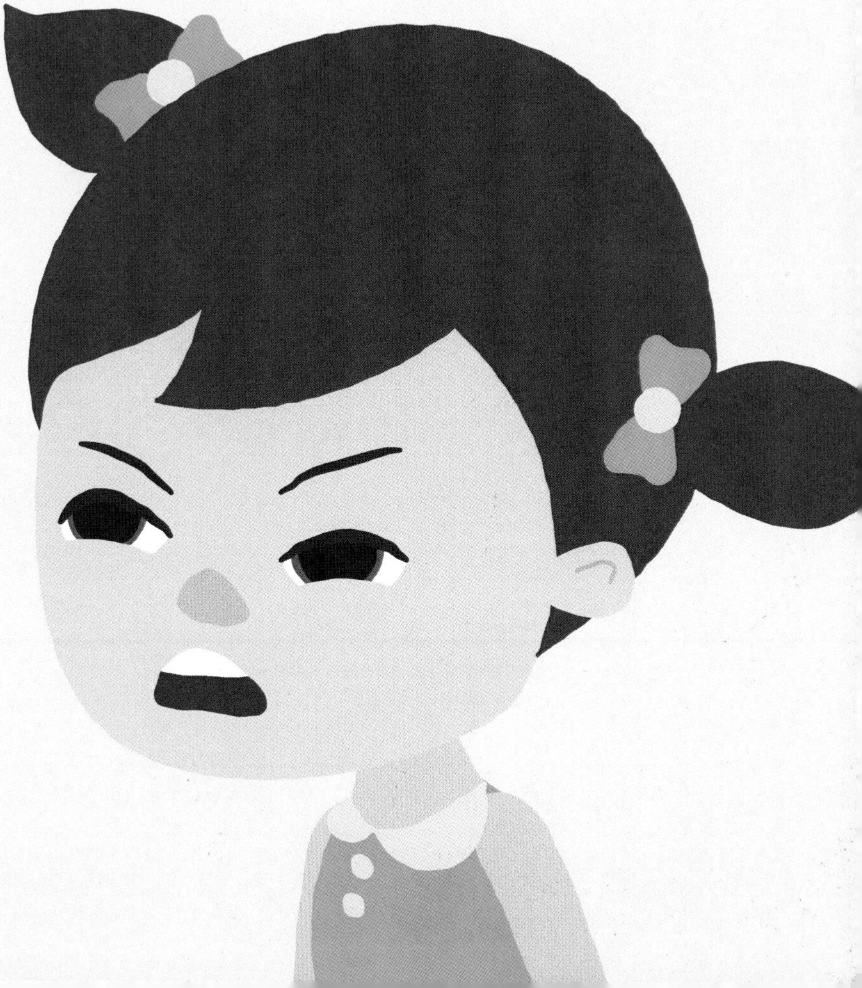

Good work!
Let's keep going.
You're doing such a
great job!
Give someone
next to you a

HIGH*FIVE*

Whenever someone touches your private parts, they have broken the Touching Rules. And you need to...

1 Yell "No!"

2 Run away.

3 Tell a trusted grown-up in your community

Who is a trusted grown-up
in your community?

A trusted grown-up
in your community can be

a doctor, a fireman, a police officer,
a teacher, a family member,
a friend, a parent, or neighbor.

Who is your trusted grown-up?

_____

(fill in the blank)

When someone breaks the "Touching Rules" they may tell you to keep it a secret and not tell. If this happens, it is your job to tell your trusted grown-up immediately to get help.

If your parents make an unsafe choice and break the Touching Rules, you may feel uncomfortable and scared.
When this happens you need to...

1 Yell "No!"

2 Run away.

3 Tell a trusted grown-up in your community

But, sometimes someone may touch your private parts and it may feel good. When this happens remember to say...

NO!

Because even if it feels good, a rule is a rule. No one can touch your private parts except you!

Sometimes your private parts may be hurt or sick.

When this happens a doctor, or your parents, may need to check your private parts to keep them clean and healthy.

But, they should only check your private parts if you are sick.

Never forget, your body is your body.

Repeat after me...

"My body is my body.
I am BRAVE.
And I am in charge
of my body."

And if someone

breaks the Touching Rules, always
remember to tell your trusted
grown-up and never be afraid to say...

Made in the USA
Las Vegas, NV
09 May 2022

48653821R00024